A BETTER SAFE THAN SORRY BOOK

a family guide for sexual assault prevention.

Sol and Judith Gordon
Illustrated by Vivien Cohen

Prometheus Books
Buffalo, NY

Published 1992 by Prometheus Books.

96 95 94 93 92   5 4 3 2 1

Library of Congress Cataloging-in-Publication Data

Gordon, Sol, 1923–
     A better safe than sorry book : a family guide for sexual assault prevention / Sol and Judith Gordon : illustrated by Vivien Cohen.
          p.   cm.
     Originally published: Fayetteville, NY : Ed-U, 1984.
     Summary: Discusses the sexual assault of children and how it can be prevented or survived.
     ISBN 0-87975-768-X
     1. Child molesting—United States—Juvenile literature. 2. Child molesting—United States—Prevention—Juvenile literature. [1. Child molesting.] I. Gordon, Judith, 1923–   . II. Cohen, Vivien, ill. III. Title.
HQ72.U53G67   1992
362.7′6—dc20   92–8033
                                                                                            CIP
                                                                                            AC

Printed in **MEXICO** on acid-free paper.

A BETTER SAFE
THAN SORRY BOOK

Sol and Judith Gordon

Illustrated by
Vivien Cohen

A BETTER SAFE THAN SORRY BOOK

Sol and Judith Gordon

Illustrated by Vivien Cohen

Most of the time
it's fun
to be a kid.

You play a lot,
go to school,
make friends,
and visit
with relatives.

Maybe, Mom or Dad
takes you to the
zoo or park.

Sometimes you like it best when the whole family is together eating hamburgers and french fries.

Isn't it great when your Mommy or Daddy
or your grandparents hug you because
they love you and
you love them?

But
sometimes
bad things
happen.

You feel sick,

you fall and hurt yourself,

a bully hits you, or

something scares you.

Sometimes real bad things happen to kids—
even to the best kids.

You could get very sick and have to go to the hospital.

This can be
scary at first,
but then you'll
meet the doctors
and nurses who
want to help
you get better.

And your parents
will be there to
help, too.

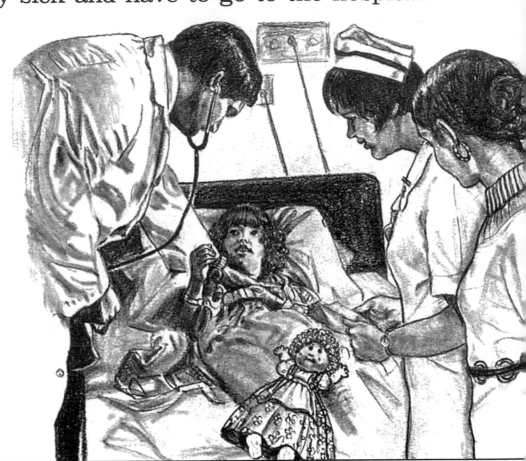

Do you know what you are supposed to do when something bad happens?

You tell someone you trust, like a parent or a teacher, and they will help you feel better.

This is because they care about you and want you to be safe.

That's why
they tell you

to be careful
when you cross
the street,

to wear warm clothes
when it's cold

and NEVER
to go anyplace with strangers.

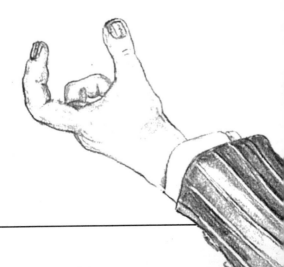

If someone you don't know wants you to get in a car,
   DON'T!

Say "NO!" and

GET AWAY,
RIGHT AWAY!

A stranger may want to give you candy or a toy.

Don't take it.

Say "NO!" and

GET AWAY, RIGHT AWAY!

We know it's nice
to get presents
from people you
know and care about,
like your friends,
but NEVER
take presents
from strangers
unless your
parents are right
there to say
it's okay.

If a stranger wants you to help find a lost dog,

DON'T. That's a trick.

Say "NO!" and

GET AWAY, RIGHT AWAY!

Practice saying "NO!" right now with your loudest, gruffest voice.

This is the special "NO" you use only when someone is trying to do something wrong.

Sometimes, people
you know and like a lot
try to trick you.

They want to touch
your private parts
or want you to touch
their private parts.

They tell you lies, like "It's okay,"
even though they know
this is wrong.

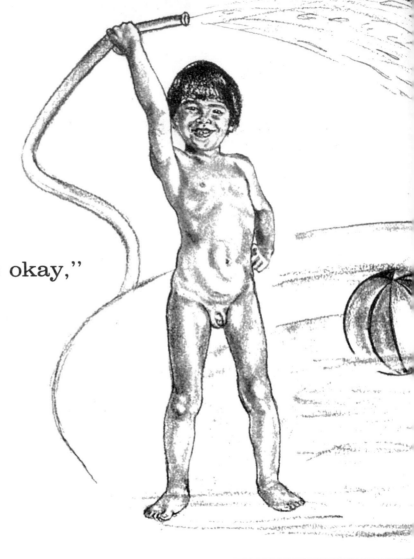

Do you know what your private parts are?

For boys, it's the penis.

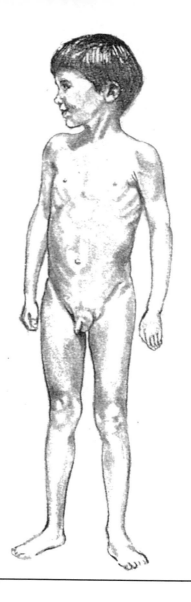

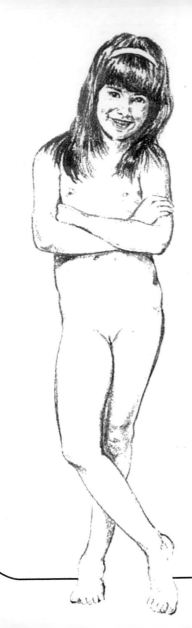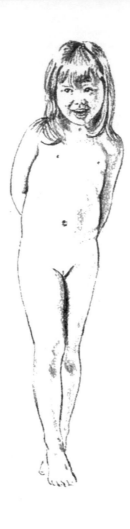

For girls,
it's the vulva,
but most people
call it the vagina.

Breasts are also
private parts
of girls.

For both boys and girls,
it's the backside
or the anus.

Private parts
are the parts
that are supposed
to be covered
when you are dressed.

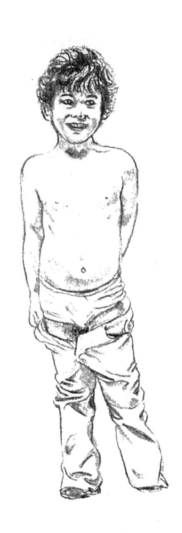

No one should touch your private
parts except yourself and you
shouldn't touch anyone else's.

Even a doctor
needs your
parent's
permission
to examine
you.

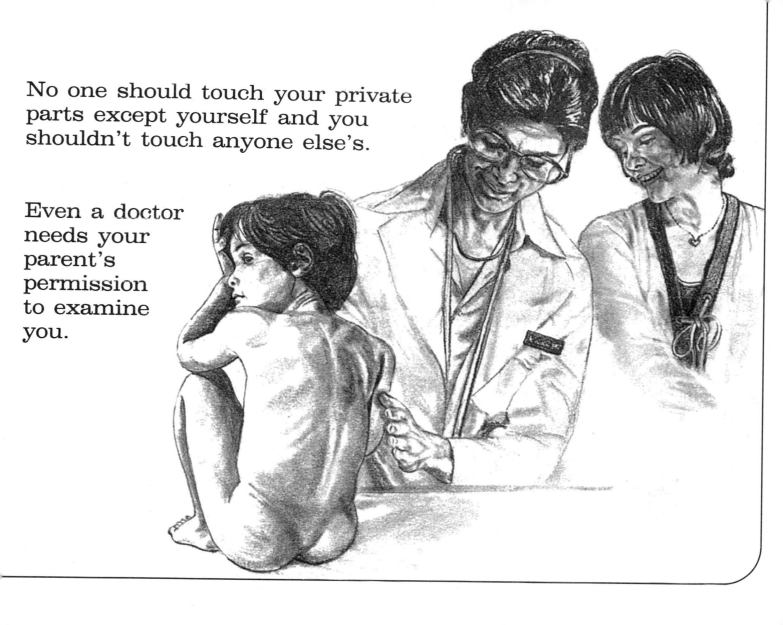

It's not right for grownups to fondle your private parts, even if they say they love you.

And it is never right for grownups to try to get you to touch their private parts.

Do you know how you can tell if someone is doing something wrong to your body -

Here's a dad tickling and having fun with his child. Tickling is fun if you like it.

But, if someone tries to play with your private parts, that's not right.

Do you know how you can tell if someone is doing something wrong to your body - even if it feels good?

You'll be told not to tell anyone.

Say you won't tell, and

GET AWAY
AS SOON AS YOU CAN!

You should tell even if you are
forced to swear to God
you won't tell.

TELL. God wants you to tell.

You should tell even if the person
says, "I'll hurt you or your parents."

Then tell.

It is NEVER wrong to make a promise
that will keep you from getting hurt.

It is also
NEVER wrong
to break
this kind
of promise.

The really bad thing is that sometimes even when you say "NO!" a grown person might force you to do things you don't want to do.

If this happens,
it is NEVER your fault,
even if you can't say "NO."
It is ALWAYS the grownup's
fault.

Tell someone you trust what has happened because most grownups are nice to kids.

Tell, even if you are afraid they won't believe you.

The person who gave you this book will believe you.

Talking about what has happened is the first thing you need to do to feel better.

We want you to know that it's all right
to tell your parents about anything.

Ask your mother or father right now
if they will ever stop loving you
if something bad happens to you.

Ask the grownup who bought this book for you something you have been wondering about.

That person will listen to you and help you if you need help.

People who love you are always ready to help.

People who love you want you to be

SAFE
AND NOT
SORRY.

PARENT'S GUIDE

Sometimes there is nothing even the best parent can do to prevent bad things from happening to even the best children. Accidents occur and deaths of loved ones are inevitable. But there are some tragic events that can be prevented; or if not, at least the consequences can be greatly moderated.

Parents have always been concerned about their children's safety, especially in the area of health and accidents. But there is at least one area to which parents used to pay little or no attention, and that is sexual molestation of children by adults or teenagers. We are not talking about young children exploring each other's bodies. As a parent, you may want to discourage this behavior, but you don't want to punish it. Playing doctor is an almost universal experience of young childhood.

Oddly enough, the worst consequences of sexual attacks upon children are related to the lack of communication between parent and child regarding sexuality in general. Without education, or what is called "rehearsal" information, children can be tricked into inappropriate behavior by adults. The question you must answer as a responsible parent is: Are you askable? Being askable means that you are available for *any* questions your children raise, especially those about sexuality.

If you can't talk about sexuality in general, how are you going to tell children to be careful about sexual molestation? While many parents are uncomfortable in this area, this does not mean you have to be paralyzed. You are the principal sexuality educator of your child whether you do it well or badly, so you might as well do it well. A list of books which can assist you is included at the end of this guide.

Children are curious. They want answers to their questions. It is simply not true that knowledge is harmful; however, deliberately refusing to answer questions children have about sexuality is detrimental. While children who get answers to their questions are able to make better decisions and can sometimes prevent bad things from happening, some children are shy about asking. If there are no questions before the age of five, such as "Where did I come from?" it's your responsibility to start the conversation. In fact, in any area of knowledge, there is no rule that says children have to ask first.

Being askable also means when your children talk to you, you listen carefully and believe or initially accept everything they say. Most children do not lie about being sexually assaulted. There might be one who does, but for every one who lies, there are 100 telling the truth. The one child who does lie is still sending a crucial message that something is wrong.

A key message of this book is that children have private parts and public parts, and no one, except these children, is allowed to fondle their private parts (penis, vulva, breasts, vagina, anus). Nor should they be asked to touch anyone else's.

It is very important to warn your child not to go anywhere with a stranger or to let a stranger touch your child's body. However, you should also know that about 75 percent of all cases of sexual abuse of children, both boys and girls, occur between children and a grownup whom the child knows well and even likes.

It is also not a good idea to put the names of your children on any of their clothing. A stranger may use the name as a way of suggesting that he knows the child.

Another crucial message is that if someone forces or tricks your child into sexual activity, the major imperative is for the child to tell someone who is trusted what has happened. When you are told, try to keep calm. Anger, of course, is a natural reaction. However, as part of trying to understand what has happened some parents say "Why did you let him do it?" This blames the child when, in fact, the child is never to blame. To give yourself time to think and, more importantly, to reassure your child of your trust, the best responses to being told are:

1. Holding your child closely;

2. Saying, "I'm glad you told me"

3. "I know it wasn't your fault"

4. "I still love you and will always love you no matter what"

5. "I'll see to it that it doesn't happen again."

Not all children tell their parents directly that they have been sexually assaulted because these children do not always know what is happening to them. What they experience is a vague uneasiness that what has occurred is not right. Sometimes children "tell" their parents they have been sexually assaulted by means of radical and negative changes in behavior, including frequent nightmares, suddenly not wanting to go outside to play or to attend school. Other children first test a parent's reaction by telling a little of what happened and omitting the most important details. Some children are afraid to tell because they have been threatened by the abuser or are afraid of the consequences, such as other people learning what has happened. If the parent's response is supportive and non-threatening, the parent will get all the necessary information to be helpful to the child.

Parents need to understand that children are afraid to talk to their parents about sexual molestation. They are afraid to tell because they think no one will believe them or because they think they will be blamed, particularly if they have gone someplace or done something they were told not to, and then were sexually assaulted. Perhaps the main concern, however, is that they believe if they don't do what a molester tells them to do that the molester truly has the power to hurt their family.

We don't always know why adults assault children sexually. Sometimes it's because these adults, themselves, were abused as children. Sometimes they feel they can't control their impulses. They know sexual molestation is wrong, but what they do not admit to themselves is that their behavior is an addiction. Besides providing children with knowledge to prevent sexual abuse in the first place, society must also convey the message to abusers that even though they have powerful impulses, that doesn't mean they have to act them out. And, of course, abusers should seek help.

More immediately, however, your concern is for the safety of your child. Being an askable parent is your first line of defense.

Children are often given little control over who touches or kisses them. How many times have you asked your child to kiss a stranger or a relative the child doesn't even know? Think about it. The important point is to make a distinction between what you ask your child to do in your presence and what someone else asks your child to do without your consent.

Another aspect of safety is to train children to be observant. When you are grocery shopping, for instance, make a game of their noticing what people look like, what they are wearing and how old they are.

Have your child memorize your telephone number and address, and then have them tell you what they are several times over the following weeks. This is information every child should know.

Play the game, "What would you do if . . .?" It's surprising how many children feel they can outsmart the adult who is out to harm them. Children need to know that there are times in life when you simply do not take chances.

We recognize that we do not meet every child's needs in this book. You may have to make a distinction between secrets and surprises or you may have to explain the word "fondle." You may have to add that adults who love each other do touch and fondle and that it is different when both of you are older.

Sexual assault is an important issue and should be discussed. This doesn't mean, however, that touching should stop. It is very important for children to be cuddled, kissed and hugged in addition to being enjoyed, appreciated and believed by their parents. For those of you who are concerned, we wish to stress that it's really not difficult to make a distinction between loving touching and exploitative sexual manipulation of children. People who sexually exploit children also deliberately avoid discussions about sexual molestation.

Parents who contribute positively to the well-being of their children are those who are askable—about anything. They know that it is ignorance, not knowledge, that is harmful. They are parents who want to help their children grow up to become healthy adults, too.

RECOMMENDED BOOKS

Raising a Child Conservatively in a Sexually Permissive World by Sol Gordon and Judith Gordon. A book that provides parents with sound advice and good sense.

The Silent Children: A Parent's Guide to the Prevention of Child Sexual Abuse by Linda Tschirhart Sanford.

Did the Sun Shine Before You were Born? by Sol Gordon and Judith Gordon. A sex education book for children aged 3 to 7.

Girls Are Girls and Boys Are Boys - So What's the Difference? by Sol Gordon. A sexuality education book for children aged 7 to 10.

"Come Tell Me Right Away" by Linda Tschirhart Sanford. A positive approach to warning children about sexual abuse (pamphlet).

"Strong Kids, Safe Kids." A home video cassette produced by Paramount designed to be watched by parents and their children. Moderated by Henry Winkler. Available in VHS and Beta Max. It is outstanding and highly recommended.